SAD ISN'T THE COLOR OF THE DREAM

- Stride -

Other books by the same author:

With House Silence (Stride)
Loss Prevention Photograph, Some Pencils And A Memory
Elastic (Tape Books)
This Stem Much Stronger Than Your Spine (MAF Press)
The Truth Right Now (Bahktin's Wife Publications)
Virtuoso Bird (Brushfire Press)
Late Summer (Pierian Press)
Memory Transposed Into The Key Of C (Mockersatz Press)
Appropiate Behavior (Abbey)
Obeli: 21 Contemplations (Pygmy Forest Press)

SAD ISN'T THE COLOR OF THE DREAM
Sheila E. Murphy

Sheila E. Murphy
SAD ISN'T THE COLOR OF THE DREAM
First edition 1991
© Sheila E. Murphy
All rights reserved

ISBN 0 946699 93 3 *(paperback)*
ISBN 1 873012 08 X *(hardback)*
Cover design by Rupert Loydell,
original collage by A.C.Evans
Design by David Goodchild

Acknowledgements:
Paper Air, Rhododendron, The Raddle Moon, Ostinato, Hayden's Ferry Review, Hot Flashes, Panoply, Lost And Found Times, Salt Lick, Chiron Review, Aerial, Contraflow, Poetry Halifax Dartmouth, Third Lung Review, Red Eye, Generator, Heaven Bone, The Plowman, Nightmares of Reason, Offerta Speciale, Edge, Chow Chow, Black Bear Review, Parting Gifts, Tin Wreath, The Wide Skirt, Truly Fine, Sonoma Mandala, Cicada, O.ARS, Fell Swoop, Conspiracy of Silence, Stone Country, Interstate, Sequoia, Tsunami, Big Allis, and Pembroke Magazine.

Published by:
STRIDE
37 PORTLAND STREET
EXETER
DEVON EX1 2EG
ENGLAND

Contents

I'M BEST AT PLAYING THE GAME WHEN I'M NOT PLAYING THE GAME

The little crevices
To go in
And out of

Punctuate a legacy
Of ghetto living

Seethe and slaughter
Chaperones in the value-laden
Forum of civics class
And speculum

Behold
I am not interested
In shirt tail connective
Tissue between my psyche and someone's
Creative imagery
Of the cosmos

Talk to me about original mistakes
Resplendent with humanity
A dither of fastball
Derivative conversation
Lathering post-haste minutia
In uniform trembling

Brass aglow
With pomp encrusted
Shorelines
Granting immunity
To self-importances
Arraigned in their composite stable

A PORTRAIT OF BEVERLY C.

There is too much to tell in one sitting. She is not sitting she stands with her t-shirt from Harvard too large that just fits. Dipping fruited yogurt from white styrofoam on Sunday. Reading ads from Target.

Every genius needs a balance to be balanced. She is she and I observe the balance in an afternoon. Wheat in July corn in July fresh artichokes. What were we talking about.

Money for a little while. She's eating with a silver spoon from the Edna Doyle estate of which she was recipient of six silver spoons. One for ice cream and five others for the storage shed.

I ask her anything about tomorrow she says probably. And I agree having no choice except to open doors leaving a place. I place my interest extracurricularly in her face and small bones my curriculum. A xylophone of much discrete music with discretion also. The crevices between equally musical. Movies to be made and lived and made.

THE GOD

A multiverse in transit gradually trapezes plain old warmth. If I could resist it or transcend, what would the script be. In what language. The rules of well heeled correspondence ripen. Spread the word routinely. Allow a fractured sadness to descend like rain. Across landscape redeemed. To plant a garden where limit equals some cycle we repeat. In favor of elements that return with names to be consumed. Basted with fire and spawned by need.

Window above the action, glasses insufficiently strong, presumption

JAZZ

Don't mention it   B R E A T H E

peace-and-quiet symptons   overflow

(card catalogue to be dreamed)   a pill down

happenstance   wrap bandages

around each moot particular   unglaze

light over suspended truth   whose

conversation mimics closure like the siren

promenading through

bait parks jostling fate

as color you could chastise

and then change

SUNFLOWER

Large enough to capture light a physical wheat orange.
Maybe functional or just a pool of useless in the yard. Curled
petals veer from center flower padded like a sponge. Heat
toughens everything about the fat weed with a face. Too large
to touch. No longer pretty like a woman once. Slum jewel.
Exempt that is to say from blades. Not lens or paintbrush.

Breath, emerging rainless life, collected

SOME YELLOWS, SOME DARK BLUES,
A CHOCOLATE COLOR

Bankruptcy is full of elbow room

He decided to declare war
On boredom before depleting
His supply of energy

The radiant intrinsic value of relief
Comes as an unexpected house guest each year

Each year we learn what mountain we are climbing

Some of the shadows want to trade
Their symptoms for the sun

Each one a separate rosary bead

Each one a story of defection

Until the floor is less a safe place
Than a state of mind

Risk fluttering like wings
Tuned in to natural engagement

Some yellows some dark blues a chocolate color

Recall that any limitations can be danced to

In the time prescribed

Recall that pantomime detracts from love of music

Snow an afterthought, some built-in safety

FLOW

"Leger" a word in French said softly all the nasal flair of openness depressing intermediate small adenoidal barrier. A working set of boundaries. I ease into this costume and become the high achiever pride permitting purity of function that surpasses. Romp through free space names named after me. Hypothesizing angst as sheepish informality. This effortless rehearsal context of the whole. Seeing the big picture negates marriage to the beaded slim particulars right feeling and resentment. Having breathed inviolate channels. Reinforcement bothering to make something matter. As I have founded my direction. Feeding enigmatic ounces.

Neglect, the overpowering, choice whispers

MY FEELINGS ABOUT MONEY REFLECT SELF IMAGE DIRECTLY

Allergies are the first honest response to overwhelming beauty of a blossom: the system cannot cope.

Massage not only relaxes, it speaks the body's only tongue.

She lost faith in him; the dreamy look went out of her eyes. I heard this on the telephone.

I hear myself speaking quietly of missing friends before they've gone.

Propagation of the species is a prime distractor from several brands of inner genius.

The look of disappointment always singes and reflects a mother's early eye.

Streetlamp first on after sunset glows faint green.

Nothing is ever duplicated.

This letter comes to represent my sole accomplishment this day.

WHERE SHE IS LIVING NOW

It is her boat her envelope her conversation
It is pressure not to be together then
To be together
Would she listen after all these

It is her monologue her sweatsuit her brooch
The organizational chart popping
With her centered
With her sheltering

It is her command of the terrain
Whereof she speaks the language
Having moved slowly away across years
Where she is living now

It is her wonderment
Scaling unfound places gradually
Having as her mate this gravity
Continuity to lower
This body her breath
Her statuesque
Endearment to the powers

A PORTRAIT: JERRY

Always a layer of him reaching layers of me underneath accessible via liquid passing in the light we slept away. Always the underside a recreation seedy bars with porno sold from shelves below visible counter our hilarity misplaced contentment. When blurred comprehending fully. String of almosts and intelligent without a harness for the intellect of any kind. Able to take it anywhere and lose. Not knowing each other except through the veil as strange as breath a secret. Loving our breath too fuel oil totally polluting. Access to other lands with freight infiltrating emotional condition. Sanctify or something. All that we required was a room and candles all that I require now. I never knew you.

A good mood at the low low price of what it costs to buy a fifth of anything

BAPTISM

Our body joins some mind focused on unfocus beautifully circumspect. Lofty particulars hum entropic figures of speech. Measure the downside. We create. Accommodate baptismal font, robes, H_2O, all things elemental to surviving. Shucking cover in the interest of society which doesn't take to naked flesh. Enabling products to approximate again the body. Largely due to circumstance. Pavement underfoot. Studded with acorns. Jazz crackling with willingness to die.

Solemnity, oils unmixed with water, separate purities

DREAMY CHAPTERS

I equate osmosis with self willed brainwash. Place your hand here do you swear to tell the whole truth. Colorized voice punctuation emphasizes nothing-to-be-done ahead of xylophone ahead of speak your troubles one at a time into this funnel and I'll recommend a dental floss to reach impossible tight places in your mouth. The whole point of this exercise is fusion. If you say so I am listening. These several gestures vary subject matter to a coast and hear the one-time waverush be an ostinato. Grandly focusing and focused on the wishbone treatise sampling hair to find a pattern in this wash. A remedy perpetual tension. Glomming onto cavities and filling them with power until the emptiness is ritually understood.

Heroism first a given, fill-in-the-blanks as to where-when, etcetera

HUMOR

Her presence when she speaks the simple flash awareness as in camera with some pleasure. Grounded as she is and acting. Clarify and touch the scintillating fun of never lonely now and wine is no equivalent. Kindling happy porous frontispiece to warn of blessed ownership. In transit majesty and light.

Conundrum always unsolved and no anxiety about it

FORMULA

Each one works her resonance from an invented set. Like code. Drumming the right responses. As though being had wound up a machine and we were each machines. Other as the capital of evil. My fantasies arresting what he stands for. What singlehandedly I might change. Intersecting with arenas' preset fate. The program never quite discernible. Programmer under pressure to relent. The live brain. Able universe. Solo concert with intentions.

Hero chime, distinct menagerie of unawareness, cutting the cord

CONVERSION

The inventor of menus is the lively one we plumb forget we trust. Chapter two, review of literature. Requires discipline to demand, comply with that. Always antecedent genuflection. How this world occurs I principally become involved in. Dive into the genetic code. Feed off listing of motet. Until the chalice cools its purpose, breathing not a word to strangers. Whatever happens, we are thoroughly prepared, having already scribed with firm intelligence the categorical implants needed. Choice little nodules so submissive we exclude them all from recent memory. Audition for roles we play already well. Bequeathed by higher self. Resistant to conditions. In plenty of time to rebound from lit matches that invent scar tissue we retrace with poised forefinger.

List of firsts, recall, petals litter the cement walkway

THE QUESTION FOLLOWING THE STATEMENT

Mortality camps
Out on my sidewalk
A priestly surveillance
Of preambles
To control birth
Keep it haywire and random
Celebrating pearlgate
Necklace she unwillingly
Receives

The sewer words complement
Reality I'm told
Quotidien amazements
Duck under prominent
Doorframes to get through
Faking the shit content
To be acceptable

Icicles and steam impress
Upon the forehead symptoms
Of ramified zoning
To build a home per capita
To liberate the fallow
Sandtraps from their nakedness

Line segments measure
The countdown to death
I quietly
Simmer here
Arrested by mushrooms
And new construction

(GRANDFATHER AND) THE PRIESTS

(Grandfather on drivers: "Where in hell are all the damned
fools goin'?")

Priests ahead of me on the plane,
row 12 aisle seats.
Thick bibles.
Talk of missions before prayer.
Skin blue white from shaving with cold water in the dark.
Black book, upturned hands.
Bourbon, swizzle sticks around them,
Do they smell the loosening and ever wish?

(Grandfather up in the night for sips, then back down.
His own schedule. Never moved from that one piece
of land except hauling lumber.
Money from ways other than the farm.
Sheepface. Fear. Wolf dogs.
Shotgun. Survival. Soft breath.)

One priest makes the sign of the cross
away from himself
as the pilot tries to land.

(Grandfather used to call this time
"forenoon."
Before the heat of day.)

I lean on time.
Go slowly through this weather.

(Grandfather's wind-y River called "Coldwater.")

A priest's shaved blue white face.

AUTOBIO-

So many things beginning. Lines. A part of speech a glamor, glasses rolling past this room atop a cart. Percussion based and strange. To unfamiliar hearing.

She met a man who asked to see her walk. He measured and he touched and diagrammed. An instance of downfall where we are taking this. Slowly away. What are you in the mood to do.

Perceived safety an alley of good cats all belonging. Somewhere your camera poised. Relentless thirst, the artist. Homecoming everywhere. Montage. Good vintage wine. Androgeny.

My sisters win when they compete she said. No reference to other members of a tribe. My sisters learn to love she said majestically and then they lean on depth it swathes their chilly arms. My sisters are my hope she said my daughters won't exist.

And then this world, the verdict. This world montage of blood and anger rapidly depleting the supply of goods and services.

Gentle goods and services.

PRESSURE

A blue
Robin egg
I think robin
Split on
Asphalt
A car going
By some
Trees olive
The moisture
Near
My thinking
What this
Has to do
With me
A distant
Sky some
Traffic
Flute all
Lidded up
Under
The pressure
Being opened
Not quite
All of it
My fault

RELATIONS

His college sweatshirt full of digested beer pronounced itself with accuracy and discomfort. I held out my hand, not wanting to. Then went on sabbatical from thinking while he told me my life history from his perspective. I felt wrinkled, raised my left hand to the forehead. But the mask was now my face, having become the look I held inside me to define myself. His head kept bumping low doorways. Source of conversation for a while. When I'd exhausted other topics, he raised old shadows in the shape of light. "Why does this man continue talking", asked the child within me. My resistance to him was so strong, the afternoon turned to an icicle I knew I'd never be able to keep, some impossible though memorable promise.

Old country, shovel full of rocks to build a wall, loose change out of the ground

SINCERELY

Mended loose leaf shadows brain the left side

Of the road with some conundrums like

Steeplechase mortality until the populace
Stops caring for the guest bedroom perfect
For hiding wishbones behind a very stuffed
Couch with a lady on it wearing understandably
Less than everything she owns showing
Of course real restraint in typically
Genteel fashion as she was brought demurely
Into this world through purse strings untangled
In the various anxieties symptomatic
Of the failures and the crosswalks and the
Impish jargon so many conversations come to
Include beside gravestones we know no
Ancestors to be remembered by

ASPIRATIONS

I wanted to be seated at the best desk in the building to be shielded from bad news. A prime location from which mountains are so visible they look like crayon freshly smeared onto a page. I thought the view would be like reading into crystal, for the mountains are a different color every hour and I'm distracted. Quiet multiplies itself into a vast chemical imbalance where I notice everything like news delivered inside thunder. Multiple insights puncture status quo which wants to be called peacetime. Which must be taken apart to fit inside the box labeled that name.

Privacy, chapter and verse, blurred wisdom signals

A DAY

Take one like the old fashioned cigarette
From a full pack briskly tap
To release the one
You ease into your hand and light
A smoke sophisticated into slow
Seductive death that makes you
At first like yourself then
Begin to disappear but gently
As if you were deciding
Between pleasure and nonexistent
Immortality

A PORTRAIT: NORM

Proceeded to talk till I was kind. About his family: daughter a physical therapist, son religious past divorce so Norm won't live with anyone. Do I, am I married. Explanation. Norm, I go on reading. Lonely till I stop, decide it's being true to instinct not the need of looseleaf to be filled in. Liberal, gentle, cooked the meals for her through 37 years. After the medical bills, worked cheap, owns merely the microwave. Her ashes. One of his relations sent plane fare. I begin to love him. Norm the next leg of my flight leaves ground without a word. I have a father.

Temper, tempered, tempering, the mangy shedule, psyche now warm enough

ECHO CANYON

Desert grows hot even in morning. Carry water. Take the ripe endurance with you pleasure dance across the rocks encompass magnet of carved shapes approaching beauty. Traced motion legs and arms extended mind enveloping the thought of mountain. City is a wide embrace. Having in mind live music of the pressure against meaning. Here quiet minerals within stones becoming each of us.

Gesture recognition, movement, after

SAD ISN'T THE COLOR OF THE DREAM

At night when free the skin accepts
Whatever comes the swingset does not show
It moves with grace
A lighthouse fixed apart can lift to climes
Where it would be discarded

Only the deep shell of the body loosens
As senses momentarily shut down stay
Suspended
Jackhammer steering wheel and ivy vine
Pronounce the taste of night
The smell touch hearing itself think
And poised always for magic

ANN ARBOR

I live alone that is a lie.
I live in memory of the lacy scars
Repeating themselves helplessly to skin
That could care less.
It is my skin. You have touched.
It is a soiled slim room no one ever moved into.
The bed is layered in two no one
Sleeps.
No one closes eyes.
Too bright an arrangement of window. Who must have
Put it there what does it cost to live
Next to an alien who shops for beauty daily?
But our beauty that cannot be licensed
On another globe what could there be to carry
Back?

I lie here reading close to zero fahrenheit
So beautiful the moon invisible to me.
Unless in retrospect from here miles out of
The point touch. Miles
From what I'm telling you. Who are you
Equals my reason to attempt this.
And the long cool atmosphere of wool scarves
Replete with old vibrations that share germs
With strangers rehearsing kindness until
It is unnatural.

There is a book face open on the bed.
The young woman in an office asking for advice.
Plush office and control I've earned.
This is not me again. She's listening.
I hear her breathe about this blizzard

Her excuse never to leave.
The bed is a rare antique no one will buy.
And I'm not selling. Still too early to tell
Unless I capture what I have
Convinced myself is mine.

RANDOM

Real life is the open window desert lightning skinny dip at night no sunblock retin-A none of the accoutrements some miracles are downright tiring sometimes women smile too much the helpfulness feels spilled it's not our fault feedback the only dictator is puppeteering mainstream stuff that manages to resurrect itself all over coasting the globe being secreted rummaging through lives to make lines such appreciable depression sanctions honeybee appliances in brainscan like vegetable restroom of the future dimly projecting selfhood on dim witted alternatives with names with faces in no pain except anxiety they've made to replace guilt some nincompoop has likely imparted.

Chantscan, praxis, life force

ON AN AGENDA

Pleasure distracts your possible palms.
                              - John Tritica

On the receiving end of wind I fail to measure.
(Anything of light)

Disturb is rank-and-file menace and claim
Hosanna-fed intrusions gladly savored
For the coming rain.

(Pleased to measure growth)

I sort and tremble
(What in breezes moves).

Watching
The upside of the hand the force of fingers.

(Chance)

Impeccable.

SILO

Smell of old flesh, bundled missives. Here imagination taints convention. Which extracts from unknown sources patience. Comfort. Candles. Crowded streets bushels of snow. A whim of poverty impeccably presented. Dry wall, patter of thin feet. The stuff of artifacts able to cleanse the soul unlimitedly festering the obstacle-free sky. Smokestack emphemera.

Cordwood, gravy on the stove, symmetrical engagement

LEARNING TO SLEEP AT NIGHT

On impulse, we sent R____ an armadillo carved from wood and painted vibrant colors from the gallery in Santa Fe. It had snowed. I could resume my feelings about Michigan beneath layers of clothes and mild hypoglycemia engaging mostly jagged edges. That began to mean. Inside the store dark masks treated themselves to information on the faces of onlookers. Yearbook photographs experiencing mild forms of possibility. That never interfered with what took place. The saintly places and transgressions. Things to be expressed. Enormous poverty learning to traipse away with feigned abandon mimicking a carefree reflex. All the symbols: snow lacing the light of streetlamp; privacy of window; tiretracks dizzying impending progress. Favored position: night in bed entwined. Abracadabra tendencies. Filling the checkbook like a gastank and unlacing principles. Soft rendering of charity so each animal redeems the self. Rekindles membership in tribe. An energetic transfer. Wavelength. In translation. Popping seams of walls between the flow. Of smooth relationship. Maintaining healthy distance. Breathing into candle without snuffing out the light.

Simple role reverberation, words listlessly correct in nature

IMPROVISE

gelatinous one-sided courtly variations
rock my nearly parsed imagination
too near sleep

gesture handful
cab fare this close to your face
attracts me bassly
won't you fail to undermine the vast token
possibilities where a note goes next
breathing slim wheat forms
from its divisible friends the measures
dividing space and time
from phsyical experience
the vent fan in the bathroom sucks a tissue
to its square of ceiling

chime this one eventual
pristine tone where it came from
whimpering an unfamiliarity
smattering words that capture
everything allowed to run loose
in or near the center of emotion

STORY WITH DESCRIPTION

My instinct keeps rehearsing what it would be like to care what happened. Maybe a microscope. Details come flooding I cannot remember who or what is wanted why. Bus heading to galleries with only image to explode into a story if I want one. Leave flecks I will design sequence as needed. Every soft emotion in a row appropiate. The sound without a watch and calendar. The memory without an order.

Formula, predict, symbology with antlers, blindfold

A COMFORTABLE

This whose miracle
Surrounds meaning
Envelops with ink
Pages and pages at handspeed
The guard letting you in
Anyway sighing because
A lingering empathy outsmarts
The only known wind
And agrees to die
Right there before anything
Decides to happen
The conscience whose job
It is to supervise the world
Comes through with roses
In return

ARTS AND LETTERS

Allow me time I can persuade you of the impact daisies. Status quo is raging to be dead again. Again. A simultaneous nervous collapse of the least generation veteran implodes. Would berry flavor do. We're out of root beer. Once when I was alcoholic every springtime fresco drabbed intelligence until I cupped my hand around the image of the sea. Veronica your cloth your lace your purpose. Sliver of the true cross neatly inlaid in chief skin. Own mortar. Fastened brick. This chalice form of kindness. This menagerie. Such small details careen along the hybrid walkway and pretend to be anonymous. Videocam drops resonance a moment the room darkens.

Vestibule, form-fitting thought, herds carnivore around us

INTERIOR WITH EGYPTIAN CURTAIN

three fold piece including fourfold window
one of the still life grazing outside
its bowl apart also from shadow
seams of the window almost
speaking out of divergence
in the mind
(hair sample supposedly
revealing
old tense say to the meta-
experts who want now
not dead fingernails dead strands
of full brain cover
who want no flashbacks
who want however this instant
to cure this instant
blatantly cancel thereby
every future dissonant with
pure vowel sounds
drumming their fingers
on the tabletop
where the Bible sits obedient
to gravity

SPECTRUM

flecks of gentlemanly breezeways traipse the room amid
strategic open curtains fully networked with the sky

*

a man I used to know decides I am worth knowing, sheets
within his files no longer interfere with instinct

*

knowing what I know, declaring algebra the clear linear state
of mind within specific mindframe

*

tools sensitive to future growth appear forlorn in the
environment remaining

*

blistering the mind with its own leavening

*

a quiet fist collapsing in the heat, the price of heat, considering
heat's absence in Europe, across the skin, and windless

THE USE OF GENERIC MASCULINE

Her mouth and skin so beautiful
All the men especially the women want her
No better lips her skin
In confidence moves steadily
Remarks do not distract
The mouth perfectly young
Wisdom showing through her lovely eyes
When did it come
All the men especially
The women want her
How does the skin remain so soft
She is polite aloof a special animation
Silence
Mouth so beautiful
All the men especially

ONOMATOPOEIA

By midnight all the gels will be unpacked and whining the release of pressure a result of acreage passed too fast for knowing. The pastures of our lives rehearse for standing still. Then crease the frame requesting memory of plastic shadows. Timing issues meld with space. As though we can't break out of logic soon enough to speak in songs. Cool melodies declaring to each other there is room in lives. Hiking across them.

Portent, light on brick, enclosure

PERSPECTIVE

I know my lines. You know them. Listen to my lines. Tell me when I am about to say them. They make me feel good. What about you? Do you like to suffocate surprise and levitate your expectation to its rightful ceiling? From which intensity contains the power to look down and stifle a cough or a laugh or a quizzical loose string of punctuation nearly glib with fluency. Look at each word, sense its impact in the realm of touch. Each corresponding sensory equivalent. Each limb of tree. Each thin or fat perception clouded with outdoors and immediate things that distort conceptual discourse. Bonfires practice raging in the spirit world. Someone relieves them of responsibility for breaking up the paintings and the thoughts behind them. Hollow at first as Sunday prior to creation. No good excuse for rest.

Riddle and rain, a place amid survival, storms and thinking

DOVE SLEEPING IN A PALO VERDE TREE

Politics continue to outgrow me.

*

The birds, mild lumps camouflaged by green line segment branches.

*

Trees need to be transparent for us to like them.

*

This one full of room enough to grow an audience.

*

Good to feel the legs attempt connection of the street to an idea.

*

Sacredness immediately apparent, all this quiet.

*

Nest so portable, is fredom worth fighting for.

*

49

I used to talk politics to the exclusion of ever seeing the mountain, purple towards sunset.

*

Impressionism is reciprocal, a relaxed fist never mentioned.

*

They lie here amid branches, sever their relationship with movement.

*

As we walk past them, define their absence.

WHEN FEELING THE LOSS OF TIME OF LIGHT

broken silos
resist the
force of gravity past
genuflection to
what must be done
substantive issues plumb
niceness in which
mosquito light reveals
the hands and forearms just so
plainsong at rush hour
becomes catechism

slippage forewarns its gradual
demise dull shadow
framing memory as bronze crayons
empower the white page to be
ecumenical

the old man saddles the boy's bike
with his tired load the way he used to
mount a tractor sit back

hands sleeping touch this book
page at a time through information
slowly such that
barely living clocks stroll
through darkness feathery until
moon gives its tidy fingernail
to charity a dark cloud
to make better the little sky

OVERDUE BOOKS

I have come to love not having read them. The still life placed just so along my desk within the study. Darkly occupying preludes to its shadow. Many thoughts surrounding like an inspiration. Germ of entreaty blossoming near windows. Conversation piece. Gentle reminder of the possibilities forthcoming. When knowledge will appear like a desired instance of crystal. Pressure to be genuine, accepting light. The nounliness of form that genuflects to content.

Plagiarism, self-projection, one beside another

NARRATIVE

"A certain pressure will inhabit me, "she repeated. I requested that she stop. This business of infecting present tense with flagworms of what might have been messed up for good, is taming a large cut of the genius population. Who sabotage themselves before success dares crawl on its scabless knees toward the first runner-up, offering a free trial for one month at no cost. But the runner-up feels an affinity towards loss, despite proximity to winning. Lottery endorsement prescience. Who deserves freedom. Who deserves numbness. Who deserves to breathe. Whatever window crowds my office with three-dimensional murals manages to discount glycerine. The long-play Christianity that monopolizes bloodveins. "Every part of me is tired," she said. I suggested meditation, plenty light. Her bi-polarity expunged the possibility of acquisition. Confidence so much like sea. Whose broken shells reduce the feet to wounds, detract from power of step.

Baking bread, solution, a vocabulary, consenting adults

CONQUER

It could be true that work is foremost bruise. A reason champions my headlines like peach neatly though spontaneously fallen from a tree so human sized, it seems related. Why do the combs of veteran plumage raffle off emotion plaintively? Some chemistry I have entertained speaks loneliness until in contrast I am cheerful as a lamb appears to humans, dawdling over ripples in the flexing river. As though things worth waiting for are heady and feasible as the economy. Downloaded to a careless peace that seems inspired by tints of flower. Amenable to change. A windshield thrumming with bone chiseled precipitation, various as dots in a child's book.

Craning neck, apostrophe, city removed by force

PORTRAIT: ELEVEN YEARS

Perspiration is so beautiful a flower

*

I watch you breathe in sleep, the oscillating fan pushes silk scarves into an atmosphere softly accepting punctuation

*

For the first time home grows easy on the mood and spacious

*

A reflection of magnetic red rock liberty under the influence of pure will

*

I practice dropping tautness down into the face whose first emotion is resist

*

Accept making the other into an image to avoid a loneliness

*

Wallpaper taunts unformed patterns into hearing ourselves think

*

Your leg outside the comforter just temperate enough to mix
the touch for dream

*

Each object in the house beyond appearance aura-laden,
visible

*

Jaw tries to relax, the color of our walls, an undetected strand
of blue behind the white

*

Something to picture, begin a meditation

THE MAN WITH NO IMMUNITIES

The man with no immunities is telling me he hears gum being chewed by women overweight who cloud his sleep. He demonstrates for fourteen seconds then another twelve their masticating cud how it appears to him. The man with no immunities recounts fat women in stretch pants screaming obscenities across production floor. Relates the contents of a note unsigned against his windshield. Also he explains how much bare unwashed feet annoy him. How he hates to look at them and think how rude they seem how unevolved. The man with no immunities is torn between his loneliness and the quality of known conversation. The temperature numbs as night approaches then melds with the insane light autumn draining his reserve.

Learning to sleep at night without the eyes closed

SPIRITUAL

Mountain keeps
eloquenting for us,
Forecast like the pretty dirge I guess of
moments when the day's last sun
especially illumines what is
quiet later. And the force of gravity
diminishes as nothing
really ever falls. A false start
easily the truth
We worship.

PURPLE CLOTH

Your altar in the bedroom homemade paper. Happiness stands by. Attunement to this station. Needle on the dial or digital precision. That through here all would be. Audible. Awe. Of course clothing a shawl even a snowstorm. People next door whose mobiles rattle with unsettling wind. In desert traffic this cool night. Bed exhaustion. A place this near your heart. The germ. Recovering.

Sacramental mention, monolith emancipated into anything but smaller versions of itself

NOT LOVING YOU AFTER ANALYSIS

The same blue sky blues humbles
My recorded intuition
Like a soft brush
Over the immaculate
Surface understanding
The shark warning burbling its grand slam
Portfolio of abstinence
And I conclude motives in a drama
I am in unconsciously
Not my motives, not my drama
The theatre of reproduction in which
You must be royalty

For I have not spattered a white wall
With any ditto marks
Nor have I pressed my real thumbprint
Into any healing pad of ink
And made new markings
Anywhere
All my life the thumb has been enough

I take my grief outside and punish it
For being grief
Impossible to genuinely dissect
Without a microscope
A savvy instrument of power and God cake
Symptomatic of eyes that will react
To monuments as eyes themselves

The you I fracture is my name
Thus seeing double as if
Plenitude were the immaculate conception

THE PREVAILING CURRENCY

This look of chess on your solo face makes you desirable. I mean power as an aphrodisiac preempts normal gorgeous interchange between friends, if that's what we believe we are. Do you know the meaning of the word "humble"? More of an abrupt appeal to the rejection not be so vocal and echo charged in memory. Outsiders with conscience juggle the few fruits of their imagination and request solemnity about them. Supposing that the meager is deserving of your adulation of a few. A sacred overlay approximating maiden voyage living comfortably between pages of diary. Seldom viewed or quoted but threading the existence. Block letters at first. Sage selection of each word, forming a quasi-thrilling sentence to make up for emptiness about the afternoon. That you could trade with a horizon in exchange for everlasting schoolyard where you picked the teams, precluded leaving anyone for last.

Miracle, a fracture, one's own doubt, a quote verbatim

A PORTRAIT OF FRIDAY

I'm hoping nirvana will last. From tile in my bathroom unstained to the skylight and tame planets gesturing moonshine untempered and gravity. Porous elongated fritter of suffocate adjectives not day is quite blue enough. Need to be sleep to be fresh fruit and vegetables sleeping in mind. Hear the sportscar impinge upon litany silence for once my hypoteneuse tuned to be morphine or oval again like the riches. The poverty membranes the church of divine hyperventilate. Unction gravel and sing is a verb. The symphonic apostrophe stropping the singular wavelength. Bright venerable pasture loquatious cement. Pan fried trout a germane fossil Germany. Open the plex with car horn and be friendly till nightfall. The federal agents are cold they are mealy astute as young sponge.

Pieces of language in words for the simple detract

A TOUR OF GREATER MINDFLESH,
   NORTH DEMENTIA

just as soon as I can I shed these clothes

     (it was this fancy dinner he
     inappropiately
     told a joke starring
     the human female anatomy and
     co-starring peaches
     fairly bozoic in all
     respects the audience consisting
     of friends just sort of
     played along)

insousiance the difference between hardball and fast

     (at home I flip on
     the TV and leave the room
     all to myself leaving
     in the room the rest of me
     (go out into)
     the icy sound of crickets
     and reflect)

what for lack of xylophone commemoratives

     (moaning truck goes galavanting
     through the sky shoes plasticly)

humbug

     (what kind of Tuesday

the day before his birthday
the day after his
anniversary the day of his
Baptism Confirmation
everything but Holy Orders also
Extreme Unction)

it comes to all dust 'tween the fingers

rodeoplex hermaphrodite
scar immobilia lack-
luster art form grazing
in the mind of canvas)

yup says the little bank book yup yup yup

SACRAMENT

Champion do legislate wheat moon. Oval chemistry beat prickly pear from crawling on head trip. Integrates esteemed and so forth master paperweight with ships etched into silver over marble cube. Landslide gymnastics wield the planet. Highlight round excursions to the holy ghost return to double cost. Allow me hammock neatly to deplete by. See the constant fracture seam inside a cone of ivy. Brim acrobatic thumbsuck really plenary. Indulgent racketeering latest bishop underground to pieces skeptically adverb happy in sand dunes of past allegiance. Memorize the periodic table. Easy care that you could take a sponge to and all traces of this earth would disappear.

Antipathy, the bathtub handsprings, name brand drugs under the water

THIS WEEK

silence resists without my noticing
until I am engulfed in it
the softest moments shatter beautiful whole things
including sense of humor until carpet is speckled
with shards that become their own objects

maybe the inkling to free each lone fraction
from wholeness releases its gravity
maybe the way I feel about you proves that I exist
that lights above our heads are really never stars
but we require them to fill in desperate blanks
in books we carry to prove context

a sound repeats itself again until I can
release a little of myself
assuming so much life is possible this planet
each fracture in the seam of universal thinking
more than enough hurts timing of descent
one morning I look up and what has died is how I thought
it had to be

CHAPTERS

Each in turn places a new call between here and where you are, hoping to patch whatever happened then have something. Only we repeat the prior downward spiral until nearly a new basement is formed where no one wants to sleep. I don't sleep. I covet emptiness, rediscover it between repeat signs. My salvation opportunity occurred and I repressed it until anything about it etherized. Now the hell to carry all this time. And fresh attempts at gaining a momentum. Nothing after.

Synergy a squashed eclectic city read about and never felt

SELF PORTRAIT IN GREEN SILK

Friday nothing ever happens afternoon I hope the traffic gentles some distance away trapeze methinks a whee bash very sort of possible this afternoon alone time plexiglass this reputational endorsement whisk brooming giveaway dead labor to the power with a name like paw I shuck the beady limp wrist cleavage from consciousness remark upon the friendship then relinquish then retool a tool and dye appendage holy sacrifice of wasting time Snow Mass landslide amenity toward never winter numb this crash course silent wrestling this new homonym with clashing memory and silver plangent ductwork how do planes fly this afternoon I live for solitude that is forthcoming her sadness for awhile was overwhelming then I recanted it was also oval green

FIRST K

Some underneath neglects to speak of the conviction that a violation has been orchestrated on some level. Things likely to be strained if he can capture this is not the same as gloom. A way of coping is pretend instead of building safe warm brick enclosure for the coming winter. Maybe the first year without snow. Approaching depth with an eraser, hoping that performance of the psychic surgery will not remove essential personality. Will retain his sweetness I wish were contagious. This morning headache comes all growth subsides. I try to talk him into trading personalities a while that his might be with tenderness repaired.

Peace a word we read about, our habits, juxtaposing price and value

SECOND K

Fierce independence gnarled and lovely roots of Dutch Elm tree. Holy miracle of brain how personality includes dismissive sideglance that resists relating. I like myself in you enjoying. Beautiful racetrack common sense. A lottery of kingdom and your pencil traipsing innocent blue paper lines accepting. Atmosphere at once releases movement. Celebration pleasures soft in memory. Full recreation of the mind. An answer height and breadth. Release the string of chance and smile earning a life.

Resistance in the history, now picnic basket, the warm sun

LINES WRITTEN IN THE 5TH FLOOR BOARDROOM

I like my way of using
this sophisticated pen
and halfway hearing
schedules of capital
net cash flow
recalling
Boccherini's template
flute assignments
maturation
while across from me a homely tie
dark suit
boredom
picturing my pretty
yellow inconspicous
ripe car
that drives itself
a learning curve
that positively brags
past traffic
mention
and a broad allowance

REALISM

Ingest the enemy to distinguish truth from fiction. A simplicity allowing natural progression minus clocktick artificially spooning moments. Each one tapered evenly to cover what it should contain. And flow. Fullness of time and pressure evenly distributing itself, itself not a dichotomy of all-that-is-not-me and me. Rather, a book containing classics and pornography alike, containing the small arguments distilling perishables and creed. No easy outs. Sandpapering the truth away from innermost suspicion.

Clown faced adjectives that modify a seam of hurt and recklessness, the essence notwithstanding

BLUE LAKE IN THE MIND

He said go there without movement

He said the only thing holding you back is the big blood handling breaststroke screen of your internal hemisphere

He said brandish nine iron vest happiness in present tense

He said what about a movie

He said being likeable is God's right shoulder

He said your eyes dream lullaby like cake

He said I take anxiety to heart

he said welcome to management land of the vibrantly unethical dull

He said rehearse till night replaces a horizon

He said blue is inevitable memory of lake

THE SURFACE

In this room of enough men to speak the odds at least one of you lying behind teeth clenched in a forced corporate smile during the fag jokes, jokes about pink and mauve and limp wrists. How many of you hurt with the presumed consensus of mainstream behavior? The ache too much to tolerate. One of you likes raw silk against your skin. One of you wants the one telling these jokes to do unspeakably beautiful things. One of you hides behind threats of disease while lusting for a simple delicacy in some, if not all, of the men.

Probability theory, crazy glue, north magnets in a pair

THE LAST DRINK

of the night
and he is
lady crazy man
wants smoke between
her legs and
his wants moisture
to gristle inside
each tight place
prays gravity to
become dance tension
day fades into
pale desire the
shape of woman
windshield creamed with
rain like silk
vision with pain
he continues looking
seeing definitely nothing
especially if the woman
in himself swallowing
and swallowing his
hatred disguised as
admiration need desire

FORMULA

Each one works her resonance from an invented set. Like code. Drumming the right responses. As though being had wound up a machine and we were each machines. Other as the capital of evil. My fantasies arresting what he stands for. What singlehandedly I might change. Intersecting with arenas' preset fate. The program never quite discernible. Programmer under pressure to relent. The live brain. Able universe. Solo concert with intentions.

Hero chime, distinct menagerie of unawareness, cutting the cord

PENCIL

Semantics is not the price the verdict or the chore precisely. Marginalia the true motive entity. A pair of glasses turned binoculars. Brown leather chair. While tethered the conclusion. Greetings from Yuma before a praline cocktail. Slim beer furnishing the entertainment. Pure meander feisty want the bungalow. Wheelbarrow full of blankets waiting to be saddled. Humble toil hot seat. Rigid orange proffering mild pudding in the yard. To celebrate vernacular. As though psychiatry wounded pillow for availability. What shield was there knowing the business knowing sheets pale blue with some chilled light. Tossing differences like salad in a bowl.

Mind flames, gray tile, a vacuum

SONGSTER THOUGHT

ever the effusive symptoms crush
lateral blather for a change
connective tissue badinerie
listen to me Bach face can't you correctly
estimate for once your true picture
of my forward crawl past the duplicity I venture
to lean ahead all statuesque brusque
teeming

the force of strange is meant
thoroughly like language
bristling with meaning
close to every valid text
we nestle and then breathe

heartily the vantage point denudes
whatever picturesque vision of health
the gurus save till last in the bleat
to buy and sell heaven like an acre
branded with savor

when things fall how powerful
will be your arms
I keep venturing to myself past all this
lateral thinking geared
to make me always A-positive
within easy access of a hospital
replete with moans and the supplies
I fantasize
when dreaming runs a little thin
and there is waste everywhere
within my thinking

GROWTH

To mute all feeling. Reach the absent figure rain. More recitation than shared speech. What she looks like. Stretch abundant fracture. Stipend wings evolving bloom. Amazement. Monochrome infected by the wizened need.

Higher learning, breath, a radiation

AXIOLOGY

cointrick directs the eyes
some lavender dance rear admiral
side to side in question
no I don't recall that must be what I said
would you repeat I do not
recollect

plumb furnace tuckered with space heat
season on its axis
silently portends
idem the next the nexus
quantum plunder

we have counting to do carefully
limited by craft of scaffolding
that hovers where eyesight would
preside

the alabaster and enormous craft
inflated sentiment
a slim boat path
through the water
someone's mother drinking on the boat
tossing her empty glass

CURFEW

Dreaming of bone
Whitened dysfunctional
As a chilled interview
The company of personality disintegrates
From blue branches almost Matisse
In their directness
Laced with paint no blue can quite explain
Pressure removed from objects of desire
I stand out on a balcony
Whistling some bastardization of a classical number
When along comes wind to displace
Any credibility I might have in the music world
Insisting cocktail napkins
And all trappings of festivity
Be lifted and leave room for birds
With simple thinking vested in their crested heads
Boistrous as single issue politicians
Threatening all the time to sue or march
Relinquish any semblance of propriety
The first order of business
Wearing permanently lenten vestments

SO MUCH GHOSTED VARIATION

So much ghosted variation entrusted to the care of dictionary mulch, a speaking part as liquor finds its way straight down. Don't mention red suspenders, wild swans, any portion of the document I sing in private. Concerning neighbor's little girl too central in my guarded life. Whose quiet halo gray is merely frost wearing the look of origami late November held to windows. A mind so vulnerable you'd want to take it into reassuring hands, to break the stride of co-dependence, keep it marginally breathing. Seated in the road holding a crash totally responsible for any cracks appearing in the covenant.

Cello wedged between unshaven knees, the dry tones known as outcome

PORTRAIT OF THE OTHER

Adequacy teems intimidatingly
I lapse watching
Where I have not advanced
The lingering illness of non-penetration
Dagwoods upon spokes
Twisted   engaging
Like the flash of sword
In microscopic shards
Bristling under skin
Tinged entropy

My guard down
I fly in the face of every wit
Celebrate defeat
Infuse sensation
Defuse sensation
Wither

The El Dorado in the left lane
Practicum
Slashed garbage
In the trough
Dutifully pressures
To impeach duties
Impeach the status quo
Formulate Ides proliferate
Old teachers write to me
Asking remembrance

The paint I use is flawed
Gunmetal color to arrest

In paintings on the page
The father
Who bristled at discovering
I did not begin as an adult
With power to relieve me of my childhood
Bruised this face
Made spitshine of my attempting

POSSIBLY VIOLET

Here her ankles start to twinge. The way the radio depicts them. A metropolis of women like this reminiscing. How he held her moving over pale linoleum. This last breath evenly distributed across her life. What she will wear when dream recurs. Possibly violet or the gauze white motion of their arms. No one is watching. Breath transposed. If there is music circling. Verb dance the true home a closure. Wheel separation in the building fastening some pages of their life to other pages. Woven alcohol just simple. Picture of its own volition seemingly returns. A boat across this water. A country to preserve an altitude. A landmass to be music I commune with sound sense feasting. Awnings block the reach of sun. Beneath the text of feeling.

Airbrush, features, moving in a time away returning

BEDSHEETS

I learn from bird sweetly intoning chemistry is also blond. Whatever works my motto was. I heard it phrased a little way that entertained me by the mockingbird. So that enlightened paces I would lie here dramatizing happened without entering the gestures. Thomas Merton quietly helped build practical altar. Parceled his time among each part of being. Gardening a trill projected in the female olive tree shedding a song. This benediction a decision to become part music.

Once a migration now mosaic, colors in their sequence, shadows that fit

JUICE

you have it for long and then

*

basketball hoop rusted brown repeatedly comes up empty

*

salt and other spices in your figurative eyes

*

teach me to be dull a while

*

power glory roses maple sap

*

dirt road leads to dirt away from

*

window a clue to where the light is

*

the desire to be rescued overpowers the desire to sing

*

solitaire machine washable and genuine

JOY

Her facelight unconditional. Mistakes I make are jewels. She tolerates then celebrates examination of response is see the nature learning to be light. See fireworks attach to sumptous imagination. Clean waxed shining. Treefrogs in night air transposed to peace within the body. In the body song remaining after work infested leadership estranged from how the human system functioning at its own helm speaking to an interruption clearly. Pausing to take breath and become it.

Livelihood, relationship, an accidental loveliness

CIRCUMFERENCE

Write a gesture named loam havoc. Silence wandful caricature placate. Zoom lens feelgood omnivore. Entreaty. Sort. Ponder and wean. The gladiola bountiful. An each for seasons roundly shift perspective. Attitude and trench. The strata gentle honesty. To fuse themselves, be seen in the right places. Fortify etcetera replete and grandiose. Perpetual dream sequence seeking punctuation to die from. Cool night sky. Smooth gravity, scarred silent pasture.

Ease the coat on tapestry slow motion pontiff bless

MEDITATION ON IMPATIENCE

The pay channel of my productivity threatens to foreclose on
this body
Unless I lie still and render unto the world
Each vocabulary syllable entrapped
In globes of misunderstanding

What do they want of me these small firecrackers
Occupying every joint
When I move it's not a celebration of independence
My presence scuffs the paradise in which
I am an intruder
Until my brain can pacify this body
Until my blood cells can engage the flow
Not force a pinching of their space by urgency

I see a swirl like very fattening French donuts
Trying to cover flatlands of this universe
Politely as if it were possible to force a speed on God
And time creation to some criterion referenced banana peel
On which festive heels are slipping
In the fandango symbolizing
An escape from peace

90

NOTES

This vibration harmony if unison is not likely apendage. Here a silo there a thief. For once admitting invitation sacrifice. A speck of the germane until I breathe myself to happiness. Until the sacrament of copulation overtakes Madonna stores. Brands new utility to cold-showering the greed away. Barstools and formica printed handily forswear the grimace of this day. No one yet aware. The red fizz entertaining throat muscles deepen the impression. Swallowing aesthetics so bold they require a fascination with the leaves the chores the warbling folk music to which protest inevitably returns. This rampant silence until urgency takes over the desire for peace. Persuades it voice is a prerequisite. Then deepens.

Chant frame, ecstasy, the distance

PRESTIDIGITATOR, EGGCUP

Probably if you fried some circuits, then went straight we would have something. We would have some delightfully surprised rendition of "Old Man River" thumbing a ride. Thumbing his nose at polite society's backwash taboo at ever dredging something unpredictable. Is where it lives. The little metonymic pronoun we place all our bets on, hang our collective hat, perform push ups just to count them.

Scrapbook tantrum, wide waves of peace, calendula

A SYSTEM

Single minded happiness abruptly happens after I have stalked it all these years. I don't know what to do with so much light except remove from view its enemies. Pose hypothetical engagements with the only poverty available. Realize I do not need it any more than wealth. The middle ground will satisfy. Entire populations of ground zero like plantation heroes washing hands of scars from cotton husks in temporary fields. Rotated like the grainy short-term view of a success. My nature is congenial as a hoe and dirt-resistant. Though I understand its function in the human system. Planting and releasing us from planting with our bodies tuned to every element. Chained happily to conjured visions of our destiny. Hopeless as common denominators for distinguishing greatness from a plodding source of threat. A timely menace. Leaning inward, where stars fail.

Chapter, novel, language, thought

THE PATH TO SOLITUDE

Miniature genius I would classify him. Made the neighborhood impossible his mother on some deadening drug none of us understood but read about in *Newsweek*. She was interesting refined a coke mind constantly in search of funding. Meanwhile the son fed his vocabulary to a literate high school pitch that waged impressively against his five years. Took up with dog-eared little towhead neighbors renting in another building who would vandalize. We neighbors tried still to enjoy pool patio and such but opted finally for inside where no one asked obsessively bold questions. The way he looked when he would ask was hurt already. Required a fleck at least of kindness for the conscience to survive. His mother read her magazines described in convoluted tales potential funding sources. She was evicted finally. Packed boxes of refuse to replace the nonexistent furniture some skinny old white guy came helped her haul away from that enclosure powerless for 30 days or more. The window shades were left askew I noticed walking by this morning. The upstairs neighbor waved from patio as happy as I've seen her reading the paper without interference. I took down drawings he had made from my refrigerator door hauled out the trash. Climbing the mountain afterwards seemed simple. Body integrated with the mind.

Closure, the relief a genuine new chapter, breathing

AND TO DUST

M. said you write like other people till it starts to sound like
you
help I'm in this maze this one particular establishment
copy of the moon mud happenstance the truth
collaborate like a drug system of paradise
decentralize momentum scurry if you will establishment
carnivore and broccoli machine trap ecstasy brimming
with hogwash the mind wants meat potatoes the mind wants
chicken curry squeaky flagpole sunglasses an assassination
self expression the establishment a little party frock
of line breaks beaks of entry level wood carve
blanch and shuck upholstery sponge shoes
all of the necessities establishment #116 scribbled on map
we're not ever going to use stretch to decipher
nonetheless establishment l-tryptophane lining my gut
the dog the cat unpleasantness a swish of other cars
birds singing establishment the very shoes to run away

ADAGIO SILK

Not to eat cholesterol soothes fears when too long go the days
that inch down into sad protective units singly occupying pace
opting disclosure. As silence tracks germane belief systems
and guides by hand their mention. Symptoms expose their
roots to ineffectual white frames. Head pictures last forever
the original construction. Artist's breath. A life view spoken
free to touch. And when touched change. Long dirt road
forestation. Gradual watched cared for. Story of how genuine
new mind can be. Sing gently vowels worn without comment.

Mercy a commodity for once, detailing care and feeding
variables

MASS AT THE CRYPT

My father the brains of this outfit can't remember his own name or where he has misplaced the pipe tobacco matches eyeglasses the pipes themselves. A man I see at football games dispenses communion by splintering the host he gives to me. As though he's changed his mind about recipience. I say "amen" astutely as though I had just learned the word. My father takes the stairs leading to moderate bright weather. Braincells each day are dying happily within him. The daughter is prepared to be both shade tree and moonlight remedy the situation. How it works and plays.

Syllables to mean smallest prayers, the ice once broken

A DRAWING OF PEACE

This is my house in the woods that smell like growth you leave alone. My house with vines wrapped over every window brick and chimney. Inside fire contained enough to function. Cook our meals make floors easy for bare feet plant us shadows on smooth walls. Obligation not a word. My lover inside trancing magic very able hands and thinking. Always room for celebration and the sweet breath of the woods seeping through windows. Some sparks in daily living yes. Some prayer. Some wonder-what-the-next-day-brings. And peace not an uncertainty. The simple drawing or elaborate oil not laden with aboutness. Just the nouns their individuation. Just teakettle leaving trails of steam in patterns over stove. Whatever weather. Not force fitting aspects into shoes with no reason for walking. A music perfectly in touch with where the body pleasures. Votive candle seam and silence underpinning ripened conversation. Things not controlled but being consonant with other being. Justice and a spice to this not boredom. All invention generous unseating reach. The reaching not a desperate grasp for last breath. Rather the abundant store of breath trusts deeply breathing. Without the need of reason.

Chant without the noise, a coexistence, day and night

FALLING IN LOVE FALLING IN LOVE WITH YOU SYNTAX

Duties over I am
Falling in love falling in love with you syntax
Things as they might be
Once I went with sad geology
Who knew rocks not impurely
Talked of rocks touched the soul
That rocks may have
I drank a toast to new tall order
Meaning me I drank a toast
Taught him to drink a toast
Got sloshed with him
And dreamed of you prolifically
Falling in love falling in love with you syntax
Gambling away bread money
Gambling away shoe money
Gambling away approximate he-man ventures
Limited partnerships unlimited
In search of capital gain
In search of no load growth
In search of anger
Meanwhile
Falling in love falling in love with you syntax

SKY

then just a fleck of sunrise light expounding on a theory
elbow room whose justice flounders
instant buildings sequence
alloy skin pressed all across the surface
stretch athletic noun collective female breeze
extending to the retina until some sparks of hearing
fortify ephemera the larks the robin season
piecemeal rain the silence
or an edge of mountain seeping
into conscious view airplane and cars
arrest the block of tandem
long apostrophe absent possessive part of speech
the park the water somewhere meanwhile surface cloud
trimester glass the finely ground attachment
penciled to the very power of sight